YOU MIGHT BE FROM TEXAS IF...

Nick Anderson

MacIntyre Purcell Publishing Inc.
194 Hospital Rd.
Lunenburg, Nova Scotia
B0J 2C0
(902) 640-3350

www.macintyrepurcell.com
info@macintyrepurcell.com

Printed and bound in the USA by Bang Printing.

Design: NickAnderson
Layout: Channel Communications and Alex Hickey

Library and Archives Canada Cataloguing in Publication

Anderson, Nick, artist   You might be from Texas if... / Nick Anderson.
(You might be from if...) ISBN 978-1-77276-006-4 (paperback)

1. Texas--Social life and customs--Caricatures. 2. American wit and humor,
Pictorial. 3. Comic books, strips, etc. I. Title.

F386.A54 2016   976.4   C2015-908039-8

For my boys, Colton and Travis
(whose names, incidentally, are hidden in each cartoon)

FOREWORD

You might be from Texas if . . .

    . . . you don't mind outdoor sports in heat hot enough to roast a wild turkey.

    . . . none of your Longhorn and Aggie *compadres* know that you're a secret Ohio State Buckeye football fan.

    . . . you're a transplanted Midwesterner with a knack for drawing, an eye for tradition and an authentic sense of humor.

Of course, if you're *Houston Chronicle* editorial cartoonist Nick Anderson, you're all of the above. And more.

His latest book, *You Might Be From Texas If . . .*, is a pithy collection of cartoons that pokes fun at everything Texan—from our adoration of guns and hot sauce to our uncanny ability to properly pronounce *Refugio*. (A hint: replace the *g* with an *r*.)

Anderson has tapped into one of our best traits as Texans—we maintain a special brand of boastful self-confidence that allows us to laugh at ourselves. We do it all the time, especially when we're the butt of humor dished out by snide and usually envious foreigners from other states in the union. Put-downs of Texans, it seems, has no boundaries.

There's the regional slight: "If I owned Texas and Hell, I would rent out Texas and live in Hell," said the late U.S. General Phillip Sheridan from upstate New York.

There's the black-humor attack: "You know the good part about all those executions in Texas? Fewer Texans," said comedienne George Carlin from New York City.

And the jealous lament: "Like most passionate nations, Texas has its own history based on, but not limited by, facts," wrote novelist John Steinbeck from Salinas, California.

Natives and late-comers, alike, Texans even deride themselves: "All new states are invested, more or less, by a class of noisy, second-rate men who are always in favor of rash and extreme measures, but Texas was absolutely overrun by such," said Sam Houston, a Texan transplanted from Tennessee.

To the nattering from those woeful wiseacres, I can only chuckle and respond with words from immortal Tennessee frontiersman and Alamo hero Davy Crockett: "You can all go to Hell; I will go to Texas."

I'm glad Nick Anderson has come to the Lone Star State. He's a welcome addition and a fine Texan. That doesn't mean he owns cows, rides horses or measures distance on the highway by hours. His blood type isn't Bar-B-Q. And he doesn't slather Tabasco over his Cheerios.

But he's one of us, now.

And I suspect when asked what country he's from during his travels overseas, Nick proudly puffs out his chest and answers exactly like the rest of us always do.

I'm from Texas!

— James A. Baker, III
James A. Baker, III, was the 61st US Secretary of State
and is a fourth generation Texan from Houston.

INTRODUCTION

One gray day in February of 2015, I got a call out of the blue from a John MacIntyre, of MacIntyrePurcell Publishing Inc. He told me they had done several "You Might be From If ..." books in the Canadian provinces, and they wanted to do one about Texas. He said they'd been looking over my work and wanted me to do it. It would require and additional 120 cartoons on top of my day job, in less than a year. My first, reflexive, response was something like, "Nick, slam down the phone and don't answer it again for 48 hours."

But I decided to hear him out, and I'm glad I did. I've been in Texas for more than 10 years now. It's one of the most interesting places I've been, with one of the most unique cultures. I've grown to love this state, with its extremely friendly people, diversity of cultures, and geographic variation. Moving here was a tough decision, but it's one of the best decisions I've ever made. Texas is full of transplants. We all become a part of Texas, and in the process, Texas becomes a part of us. Sorry Texas. Like it or not, you're stuck with me.

This book was significantly harder than I expected. I spent many days going to work, drawing a cartoon, then coming home and working again until 1 or 2 AM. The most interesting challenge came along when my cats brought fleas into the house, and they decided to make it their home as well.

My spirit of Texas hospitality does not extend to fleas. I kept spraying for them, but they kept coming back. Unfortunately, I couldn't stop working; I would have fallen too far behind and I had a deadline. I went to bed many a night with fleabites all over my legs. I finally got rid of them after about two months of spraying the floor around my desk. Maybe I was the one with the fleas?

I have many people I would like to thank. First among them is my beautiful fiancé, Angel Drake. She looked at every single sketch before I finished it to tell me whether she thought it worked or not. She was my de facto editor through this entire process. Ironically, she was born in the Philippines, but like me, she's a Texas transplant. She's also keenly observant of her surroundings, including our state's culture. She was able to give me great feedback on whether my ideas were Texan enough. She helped me research a lot about Texas, and what the natives think makes our state unique. She fed me plenty of ideas and observations. She's also pretty easy on the eyes, so I didn't mind asking her what she thought quite frequently.

Anyone who knows me knows how I hate it when people try to give me ideas for my editorial cartoons. Editorial cartooning is a very individual thing, with a unique voice. Signing my name to someone else's idea just never seemed authentic. This book is a different story. While a majority of the ideas in the book are mine, I solicited ideas from many friends, especially native Texans. My hilarious buddy, Charles Flood, contributed several ideas. Also contributing were James Harrison, Lowell Hoover, Bill Kelly, Dave Cox, Andy Blieden, and Atif Bhanjee. Many others, too many to name, contributed observations about Texas that gave me fodder to mold into my own ideas.

A handful of cartoons in the book I can't claim credit for, nor can I trace authorship. They've become classics that seem to have been told and retold in the ranches, saloons and small town porches all over Texas for generations. They've become a part of Texas lore, and I didn't want to leave them out.

I'd also like to thank Michael de Adder, one of my Canadian cartoonist comrades who has done several of these books up in those parts, and helped inspire me to take on this project, and advise me along the journey.

— Nick Anderson

YOU MIGHT BE FROM TEXAS IF...

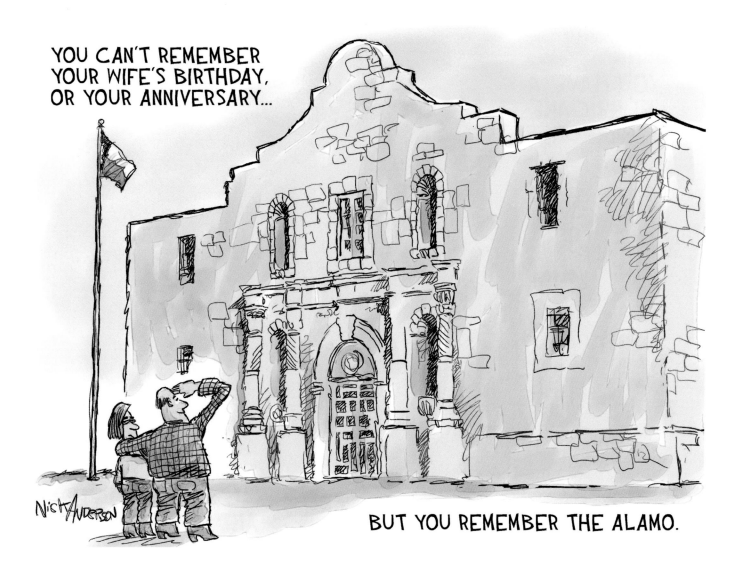

THIS IS NOT A
STATUS SYMBOL...

THIS IS.

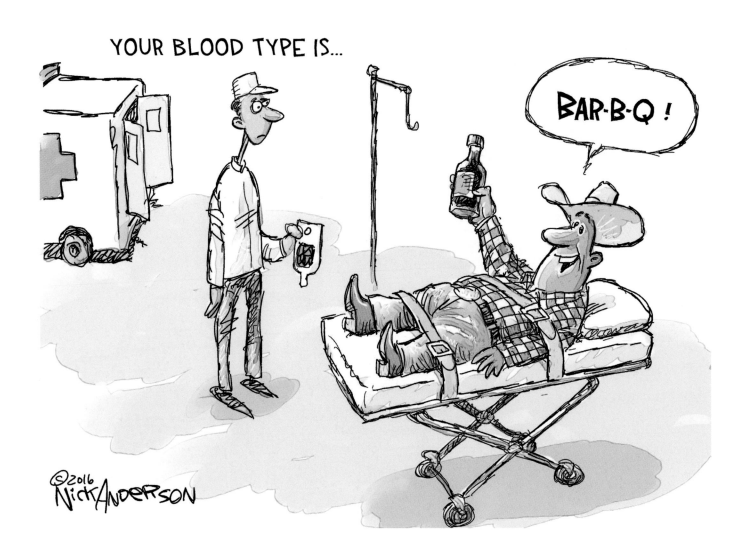

YOU'VE GOT MORE
SWAGGER THAN
JOHN WAYNE.

YOU CAN TELL A ROCK FROM AN ARMADILLO AT 300 YARDS.

YOU'VE WORN COWBOY BOOTS AS SLIPPERS.

YOU'VE BEEN CLOSE ENOUGH
TO AN ALLIGATOR TO LOOK HIM IN
THE EYE (AND REALIZE THAT'S
PLENTY CLOSE ENOUGH).

AND YOU PREFER TO SEE THEM ON YOUR FEET.

YOU KNOW THE ONE THING THAT NEVER BELONGS IN CHILI

THE SEASONS ON YOUR CALENDAR ARE MARKED "SUMMER", "FALL", "WINTER" AND "CRAWFISH."

YOU'VE BAKED COOKIES
ON YOUR DASHBOARD.

YOU COULD PROBABLY GET BY WITH JUST TWO FORMS OF FOOTWEAR.

YOU CONSIDER ANY BEER FROM OUTSIDE THE STATE "AN IMPORT."

THE BLUE BOOK VALUE OF YOUR
TRUCK GOES UP AND DOWN BASED
ON HOW MUCH GAS IS IN THE TANK.

CLICK

THE ONLY CYCLING YOU DO IN JANUARY IS BETWEEN HEAT AND AIR CONDITIONING ON THE THERMOSTAT.

YOU'VE CONSULTED A FOOTBALL SCHEDULE BEFORE SETTING A WEDDING DATE.

YOU IRON YOUR
BLUE JEANS.

SOMETIMES, YOU'RE THE ONLY WOMAN IN A GROUP THAT DOESN'T HAVE FAKE BOOBS...

EVEN THE MOSQUITOES
ARE BIGGER.

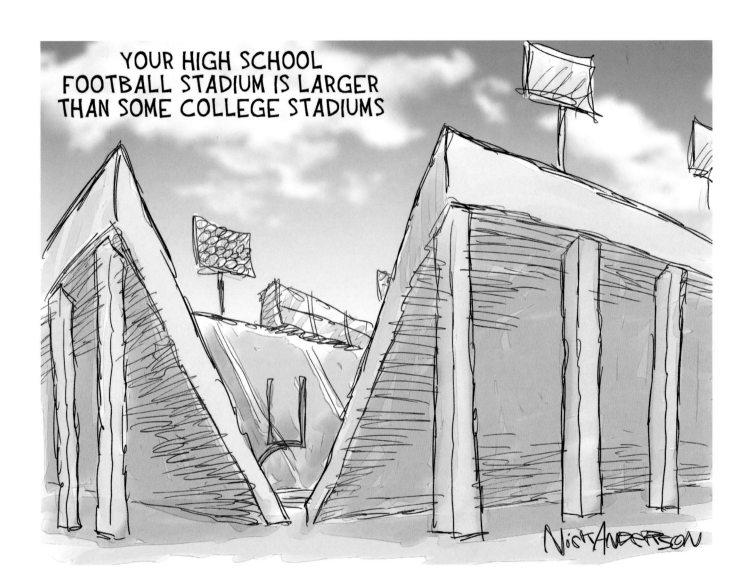

YOU KNOW PEOPLE WHO RUSH TO THE GROCERY STORE IN A PANIC TO BUY BREAD AND MILK WHEN IT RAINS.

THE BEST PARKING SPACE IS ALL ABOUT SHADE, NOT DISTANCE.

MEGA MART

YOU CAN TELL HOW MANY PEOPLE LIVE IN A HOUSE BY THE NUMBER OF PICKUP TRUCKS IN FRONT.

YOU PUT RANCH DRESSING ON PIZZA.

NICK ANDERSON

THE HOMELESS
PEOPLE HAVE
BILINGUAL SIGNS.

WILL WORK
FOR FOOD

QUIERO ALGO
DE COMIDA
POR FAVOR

YOU CAN POP POPCORN
ON THE SIDEWALK.

YOUR GUN COLLECTION IS BIGGER THAN THE PENTAGON'S.

SCHOOL GETS CANCELED FOR A HALF INCH OF SNOW, YOUR "SNOWMEN" ARE LESS THAN TWO FEET TALL AND MOST OF IT IS SAND AND LEAVES.

NO HOLIDAY IS COMPLETE WITHOUT PECAN PIE.

Nick
Anderson

YOUR KID'S
TOY CAR HAS
A GUN RACK.

YOU TAKE A DATE TO THE SHOOTING RANGE

YOU NOTICE THE WIND SOCK AT THE AMARILLO AIRPORT IS CHAIN LINK.

YOU KNOW NOT TO SQUAT WITH YOUR SPURS ON...

YOU'VE SPENT HOURS DRIVING IN YOUR CAR, JUST TO LOOK AT BLUEBONNETS.

YOU KNOW HOW TO DANCE THE "BOOT SCOOTIN' BOOGIE."

CINCO DE MAYO IS CONSIDERED
A NATIONAL HOLIDAY...

YOU KNOW THAT "CLUTCH CITY" HAS NOTHING TO DO WITH CARS.

YOU'VE PRAYED FOR THE DALLAS COWBOYS.

CUTTING IS SOMETHING
YOU DO ON A HORSE,
NOT IN A KITCHEN.

YOU OFTEN PRAY FOR RAIN...

THEN CURSE THE RAIN
WHEN IT FINALLY COMES
(AND WON'T STOP).

WHEN YOU STEP IN A
SOFT SPOT IN THE
GROUND, YOU JUMP,
BECAUSE IT'S PROBABLY
A FIRE ANT MOUND.

Nick Anderson

YOU CHOOSE A JAR OF SALSA AS CAREFULLY AS ANOTHER MIGHT CHOOSE A BOTTLE OF WINE.

YOU'VE EATEN SOME KIND OF RANDOM JUNK FOOD, DEEP FRIED TO ARTERY-CLOGGING PERFECTION AT THE STATE FAIR.

HOT WATER COMES OUT
OF BOTH TAPS.

YOU ARE AN OBSESSIVE
AND LOYAL FAN OF
A HIGH SCHOOL
FOOTBALL TEAM.

THIS IS YOUR IDEA
OF A FOOD PYRAMID.

YOU'VE EVER
MADE FRITO
PIE IN THE
FRITO BAG.

YOUR WEDDING WAS
CATERED BY WHATABURGER.

YOU'VE TUBED DOWN THE GUADALUPE RIVER

AND THE ONLY THINGS THAT DROWNED WERE YOUR TONSILS.

YOU'VE GOTTEN FROSTBITE AND SUNBURN IN THE SAME WEEK.

YOU CHECK THE WEATHER FORECAST BEFORE SELECTING AN OUTFIT.

YOU'VE EATEN FOOD IN THE SHAPE OF YOUR STATE.

YOU INSTINCTIVELY GIVE A "STEERING WHEEL WAVE" TO EVERY PASSING VEHICLE ON A TWO-LANE HIGHWAY.

ANY DAY WITH
HUMIDITY
OVER 90...

IS A BAD
HAIR DAY.

NickANDERSON

THE COWS AREN'T THE ONLY
THINGS WITH LONGHORNS
IN YOUR TOWN.